T0149631

A Timely Revolution

A Collection of Verses

LEONIE J WOODHAM

BALBOA
PRESS

A DIVISION OF HAY HOUSE

Balboa Press books may be ordered through booksellers or by contacting:

Balboa Press
A Division of Hay House
1663 Liberty Drive
Bloomington, IN 47403
www.balboapress.com.au
1 (877) 407-4847

Print information available on the last page.

ISBN: 978-1-5043-1263-9 (sc)
ISBN: 978-1-5043-1264-6 (e)

Balboa Press rev. date: 04/04/2018

Contents

A Timely Revolution

As the second hand ticks round the clock sixty times every minute,
A revolution started, but we didn't begin it.
It started itself because it was the right time
To move on from this world's chaotic paradigm.

As the minute hand rounds the clock sixty times in an hour,
The revolution grows. Do you feel its power?
Momentum increases, heads and hearts begin turning.
We look for a new world as the old one starts burning.

As the hour hand goes round the clock twenty-four times every day,
The revolution unwinds; please don't stand in its way.
No-one can stay and ignore the onslaught.
With eons of planning, our souls have been bought.

As our earth spins each twenty-four hours towards the sun then away,
At each revolution there comes a new day.
Why has it taken till now for us to finally see
That for us to continue this way just cannot be?

As the moon circles the earth and another month passes,
The revolution progresses. We should all raise our glasses
To say goodbye to the old world, our old training ground,
And welcome the new as its turn comes around.

As the earth orbits the sun and creates all the seasons,
The revolution continues and for very good reasons.
Our world is worn out; its time's at an end.
Not even renewing our thoughts will help it to mend.

As our body-clocks advance through another decade,
All our old cells have died; we have been completely remade.
The earth is a cell too; it is being gradually replaced,
Like the old cells in our bodies, it will soon be erased.

There will come another, an earth all shiny and new.
But before this can happen, our hearts and minds must change too.
We have to decide which way we want to go.
Change will come gradually; when it does, we will know.

As the doomsday clock stands at three minutes to midnight,
Choose revolution over apocalypse, choose harmony, and choose right.
Fight for justice, equality, honesty, and peace.
But do it gently and calmly, and watch the world's love increase.

We are the revolutionaries; we have the power.
We must have no fear in our hearts; we must not cower.
Revolutions aren't easy; we must be determined to succeed.
I know we can do this, and I wish us Godspeed.

Global Storming

Somewhere in our future there may be global warming.
But right now, in the present, we are seeing global storming.
The weather is going haywire. What could be the cause?
We now know that it's our actions, together, mine and yours

The way we use the earth, which is akin to our mothers,
Is also like the way we treat our sisters and our brothers.
When greed is the emotion that is the ruler in our lives,
We struggle to stay married to our husbands and our wives.

Sibling rivalry, jealousy, and bitter family feuds,
Neighbourhood disputes and just plain bad attitudes.
We steal from each other; we take from the earth.
We only think of ourselves; we've been this way since birth.

As children we learned selfishness, avarice, and greed.
We take what we want, not what has been decreed.
We don't plan for our futures; we want results right now.
Like spoilt kids, we can't wait, and so that is how
We have arrived at this point. Now what can we do?
Is it too late to fix us? I mean, to fix me and you.

The problems that cause earth's destruction are lurking deep inside.
Our human natures and egos, earth's harmony can't abide.
We can't get that "new thing" cos the money's all been spent.
So we "take" what we want, but still we're not content.

Is human nature set in stone, or can it, in time, be changed?
If we see that there's a problem, can the right help be arranged?
Can the earth regenerate if we improve how we use it?
Or has the problem grown too big for us to try to diffuse it?
Will we ever get the chance to go back to the start?
Before we try to go back, let's first fix our heart.

Time Saving

If there seems too little time to do all that you planned,
Observe daylight savings; it might help you understand
How borrowing from Peter to pay Paul can work quite well.
Shifting time forward or back does no damage that I can tell.

If we can loan the light to the dark end of the day,
So we can get more things done and have more time to play,
We should be able to do the same with time quite easily too.
Just get up earlier every day and have more time for you.

No need for you to lose sleep; turn in early, and you'll see
How much time you can save by not watching the TV.
In the morning, do the things you said you'd do if you had time.
Have brekky, get organised; slowing down is not a crime.

Relax, read a book, spend some time with a friend.
Enjoy the time you have right now; that's what I recommend.
Our self-worth should not be measured by how time poor we are.
Spend your time more wisely, and you'll see you can go far.

A Leader

A leader must be organised.
Have clear rules and boundaries set,
And consequences put in place for when
His standards are not met.
A leader should be firm but fair.
He must be prepared to follow through
If someone steps over the line.
His colleagues will expect him to.

To earn respect from those he leads,
He should show respect to those above.
As he sows, so shall he reap.
That is the universal law of love.
His position is one of trust.
He cannot take; he can only give
He must suppress his own desires.
His ego must die for him to live.

I Am Not An Expert

I am not an expert, but I know a lot of stuff.
And as I age, I realise I will never know enough.
There's always more I want to learn, more things I need to know.
Like where do our thoughts come from and to whence do they go?
Are they floating round in space, just waiting for the time,
When they can float right back to us if the time is prime?
Then do we have déjà vu because we thought that thought already,
And if they all came back at once, would that make our minds unsteady?
And where do our phone messages go when they are not received?
Do they sometimes get mixed up with thoughts; can the thinker be deceived?
I know this all sounds complicated; that's why I need to know.
Did Mr Marconi allow for this when he invented the radio?

Ode to Poets

A story told in prose uses far less words than those,
Written in paragraphs and chapters.
When a poet uses rhyme, the result can be sublime,
With the lyrical colloquy that it captures.
Poets search within their mind, each perfect word to find,
That which best befits the image they're creating.
They paint with careful strokes, on the very heart of folks,
To ensure their story won't need annotating.
Wordsmiths they must be, with an inbuilt dictionary,
To artfully convey an impression worth the sharing.
To delight and to amuse, they must very carefully choose,
Their thoughts and words so you won't lose your bearing.
Every stanza that they write, to engage or to delight,
Evokes emotions that are subtle yet compelling.
Each carefully worded verse serves to totally immerse,
The reader in the tale that they are telling.
A book enthrals for days, it can enlighten and amaze,
A poem does all that too but so much faster.
As an artist, a poet, although you may not know it,
Is undoubtedly and deservedly a master.

Privacy

I meditate every morning; it's the most peaceful time of day.
I value this time of quietness, so if there's something you'd like to say,
Please respect my privacy and leave me undisturbed.
Sometimes interruptions leave me feeling a bit perturbed.
Write it down on paper and we can talk about it later.
If the matter to you seems urgent, and you feel your need is greater
Than my need for peace and harmony, then you may seek assistance.
Please prepare yourself however, to encounter some resistance
Generally, I'm much too polite to say what I am feeling.
Any form of anger, to me, seems so unappealing.
I'm sure you get what I am saying, so we need not speak of it again.
Now get yourself back to work, and leave me to my Zen.

Success

I have read a lot of self-help books to help me find success,
To build a better business, to grow wealth, and to worry less.
But what does success really look like, and how do we define
If someone else's version is more effective than yours or mine?
To a single mum with lots of kids who struggled on her own,
It may be seeing her kids are happy now that they are grown.
To a businessman who loves his job, perhaps he'd be content
To know his customers are happy and that he can pay his rent.

Not everybody wants high-stress, lucrative employment.
Some may prefer to work less and have more time for enjoyment.
A bigger house, a faster car, or new and stylish clothes
May make us look successful, but what does it cost us to get those?
Do we have to sacrifice our health in order to get rich?
Or perhaps compromise our values if we're tormented by the itch
To appear better than our neighbours and more impressive than our peers.
Will we look back with pride on our achievements, in our latter years?

To understand what success is, we need to take a look inside,
And work out what it means for us and let that be our guide.
We all want different things from life; we all have different needs.
The one who walks his own life path is the one who most succeeds.
The self-help books that I have read brought success to their creator.
They worked diligently to produce what became their own wealth generator.
I purchased some to work out whether theirs might work for me,
And in the process, I helped them get what they needed. Do you see?

The cycles of life and of water

As I paddle down the snowy river
Metaphors wash into my mind,
Of the cycles of life and of water
Which are really two of a kind.

We are all but droplets of water
Journeying down the river of life
We're all heading for the eternal ocean,
But on our journeys we must overcome strife

At times we come across rocks,
Which slow us when they get in our way.
Just as in life there are small problems
To be dealt with every day.

No rocks can ever prevent us
From continuing our journey downstream.
We can go under or over or round them,
They may slow us but can't end our dream.

Our journey may be a long one
But it's broken down into bends.
We see only one bend at a time
This helps us endure till the end.

If we could see the full length of the river,
And every obstacle that may slow or impede.
It could prevent us from ever beginning,
And so then we could never succeed.

Our journey is not always easy,
We face many challenges along the way.
Whether it's deep or it's shallow
Hot or cold, rough or smooth, who can say.

When strong winds blow we push harder,
So we don't lose ground that we've already travelled.
When the winds at our back we can rest,
And float along as the view is unravelled.

The urge to flow downstream is so strong,
It requires too much effort to try to stay here.
It's our nature you see, to flow down to the sea,
When we're in flow we feel much lighter and freer.

Often diversions can occur in our travels,
That can hinder us from reaching our goals.
Water could be trapped in a tank
And be used to wash up someone's bowls.

We could be flushed down a toilet,
Or used to irrigate a crop.
Or polluted with toxic chemicals;
Should these diversions cause us to stop?

Worry not little droplets of water,
Wherever it is you get lost,
The sun is your friend he will save you.
You can evaporate up to the clouds at no cost

There you'll be purified of all the toxins,
That polluted you when you were here,
To fall again clean and fresh from the clouds,
To continue your journey; have no fear.

Likewise in our journey as humans
Do we suffer the same kind of fate?
If we're diverted somewhere in the middle
Can we resume? Is it ever too late?

What if our lives end too early?
Do we come back and live them again?
Will we remember our previous learnings?
Do we fall back to earth again like the rain?

What if we are like droplets of water?
And the cycle goes round and round.
Water's in the oceans and rivers
In the clouds, in the trees, in the ground.

Maybe we would come back different.
Perhaps we've been here before.
So many questions to which I seek answers,
So many possibilities to explore.

There is only one way of knowing,
If this hypothesis could really be true,
And that is to continue on my journey,
And enjoy each day till I do.

The seasons of life

Autumn, the season for changing colours and letting go.
Our children grow up and leave home and we let them do so.
Like leaves they blow around in the wind for a while, lost, finding their way.
We become like the bare trees that let them go, we feel naked,
Separated from our leaves.
Winter comes, we feel cold, and our world is grey.
The wind howls, or is it us.
Just when it can't get any darker, the days start to lengthen.
Birds build nests, wattle trees flower.
Spring returns when babies come to visit. Little buds,
We watch with joyous hearts as they unfurl their leaves,
And grow into saplings and flowers.
We revel in their warmth.
Then the long lazy days of summer arrive.
We bake, we feed the young and watch them grow stronger.
We weather the storms of summer, unstable pressure systems
Cause lightning and thunder. It's all a part of growing up.
We watch as our children struggle with their "autumn" and letting go.
The seasons continue undisturbed.

The Spirit in Man

If I was the sun and you were a plant
Or a cow or a peacock, a fish or an ant.
You would feel my warmth as I shine my rays down
And cloak your body with a soft golden gown
Would we call sun a presence a spirit or matter?
We see it and feel it but I don't think it's the latter.
Although it touches us, it can't be held in our hand
Yet its presence is crucial for all life in the land

It helps feed the plants and warms up the soil
Where thousands of grateful insects busily toil
It gives light and heat for all who live here below
I'm telling you this because I want you to know
That although it's not matter it is seen everywhere
It permeates the land and the water and air

It is very much like the spirit that is in you and I
We can't see it or touch it but even when we die
Our spirit lives on, it has been here before
It comes back different each time so it can explore
New ways of relating and new ways of being
Of touching and tasting and hearing and seeing

We need a physical body to explore physical senses
Our learning begins when our new life commences
But if we've been here before and have knowledge inside
How do we access it and why does it hide?
Can I bring any of my prior learning to the fore?
And why does my spirit need to learn ever more?

I think for a man to return as a woman is wise
Because life is much different for girls than for guys
To experience life through the eyes of black, white and yellow
Might help to make me a less judgemental fellow
To experience poverty and yet to be happy still
Or a life of plenty where greed drives me to kill
To experience pain and hunger and cold
To mature through life's stages until one is old

To hear beautiful music and see magnificent sights
To see sunsets and sunrises and bright starry nights
To climb the ladder of success and then suffer a fall
To eat like a king and then to not eat at all
To experience all the contrasts that life has to give
Will help us to decide on the best way to live

It seems in this world everything is in a contrast
Rich and poor, bad or good, future, present and past
To share our resources more fairly, we have to choose
But there are still too many who feel they would lose
We still want to hang on and to fight to get more
Our fear of not enough is what leads us to war

When we experience such lives as our enemies live
Perhaps we will judge less and even learn to forgive
Why does it take so many lives for this to be so?
There must be a reason and someone must know
I have faith that this drama is all in a preordained plan
And the most important part is played by the spirit in man

Thoughts

My mind is like the Australian bush on a scorching summer's day,
A spark ignites and starts a fire, a puff of wind and it's away.
Try to stop it if you can, good luck with that endeavour.
As spot fires start where sparks are blown, it can race ahead forever.
The sparks are thoughts that flare up, and no matter how hard I try,
I can't quell them or suppress them;
I have never worked out why.

They go round and round inside my brain, no concluding thought ensues.
I just can't find an answer, no matter how much sleep I lose.
Instead of sleeping soundly when it's time to go to bed,
I chase those thoughts around all night, trying to rid them from my head.
Many different kinds of thoughts, worry, anger, sadness, and fear.
What will I do tomorrow, what will I do next year?

It seems my thoughts are useless, I want them all to cease.
But the more I try to focus, the more my thoughts increase.
I'm feeling so fatigued of late, in body and in mind.
I need to find a way to leave my worries far behind.

In the search for a solution, I have learned to meditate.
To clear my mind of useless thoughts, to sit and contemplate.
The workings of my body, my breath as it comes and goes.
I'm aware of each sensation, from my head down to my toes.
It helps my body to relax, and when I'm 'in the zone' I find,
Instead of useless thoughts I have more balance in my mind.

Stylish

I'm not very stylish, I don't wear make-up or high heels.
I believe beauty comes from deep within, isn't that how everybody feels?
I know that I am beautiful, because I feel it in my inner being.
I'm sorry if you don't feel the same, and If that's not what you're seeing.

I can dress up on occasion, to create a good impression.
And I realise the way we dress, is an act of self-expression.
My clothes need to be comfortable, and protect me from the weather.
The idea that "clothes make the man", I disregard altogether.

And wearing makeup on my face would only clog my pores.
It seems to have been a useful tactic for men fighting in wars,
To blend in with the undergrowth to ensure that they're not seen,
Or to look more savage to their enemies,they paint faces to look 'mean'.

But I don't intend to fight, or disguise myself in any way.
You'll just have to take me at 'face value', and that's all I have to say.
Except to ask this question. Does fashion help us to stand out, or disguise?
And why does fashion dictate that women wear heels and men wear ties?

We're all just bubbles

We're all just bubbles in a glass of beer.
It would taste really awful if we weren't here.
No bubble is more or less important than the rest.
All together we are what gives the beer its zest.
To say that we're not needed is certainly not true.
We bubbles have an extremely important job to do.
If you've ever tasted beer that had no bubbles in it,
You would have to spit it out and very likely bin it.
Bubbles add the zing that makes beer so refreshing.
Beer without us bubbles would make life so depressing.

We begin our bubbly journey at the bottom of your glass,
You will see us floating up and we might pop off as we pass.
We're ever so excited as we begin our upward climb,
To reach the top and be set free, then it is our time;
To become one with the air so you can breathe us in.
Sometimes you'll feel us tickle, on your nose or on your chin.

We're all effervescence, we are bubbly and delightful,
But please don't shake us up cos the mess we make is frightful.
If we do get shaken up our reaction is to blow,
And our bubbliness goes everywhere just like bubbly snow.

If the world were a glass of beer and the people were the bubbles,
That might explain some of our world's present troubles.
If we seem intoxicated, by the environment that we live in,
And we appear a little volatile, please just be forgiving.

We can't help but be excitable, and produce a little extra gas.
The stress and commotion seem to have affected us en masse.
The world as we know it, is a-trembling and a-shaking.
The pressure's building up, there can be no mistaking.

There must be a way you can help us reduce the fizz,
We must search and find it quickly, whatever 'fix' it is.
There isn't much time left, we can't hold on too much longer,
The pressure to explode is getting so much stronger.
I hope the solutions very near and it brings us inner peace,
And someone finds a safety valve for the pressure to release.

At last! Someone's going to drink us, they're taking off the lid.
We can't wait a second more, we're so excited that they did.
Now we can all settle down and do what we were meant to do,
Put excitement back into the beer and be a refreshing drink for you.

What is Loyalty?

What is loyalty that I should pledge my answer before I know?
I looked for definitions, but wasn't satisfied and so,
I now pose this question, and ask you please to ponder;
Is loyalty both given and received, by the responder?

Should we give it blindly, not expecting a return?
Like a loyal subject? Please help me to discern.
Am I wrong in believing that it should be a two way street?
That without benefit to both, the concept is incomplete.

I ask because I care about where my loyalties now lay.
Are they external or internal, who knows, and who can say?
Our loyalty to government, when their motives we would question.
Loyalty to a partner, when we are afraid of their aggression.
Loyalty to a football team, even when they're losing.
Or loyalty to a political party, of our parent's choosing.
What about loyalties to ideals, beliefs, and morals?
Do they sit within us peaceably, or are there tug-of-wars, and quarrels?
I'm disappointed with the dictionaries, I think this word is ill defined.
For a word with so much potential to do good or harm, I find;
Its definition sadly lacking, and some explanation needed.
I think shall just cross it out and let it go unheeded.

If you can convince my mind that "loyalty" justifies its place,
Then I will leave it in my lexicon and allow it to have space.
But at the moment, as it stands, it is not a word I'd care to use.
Please tell me, if by deleting it, what it is I stand to lose.

Catharsis with words

Feeling the hurt and allowing the feeling,
Is what I must do, to get through my glass ceiling.
Embracing vulnerability, and feeling the shame,
Instead of smothering it with cowardice and blame.

Ignoring the discomfort when it knocks on my door,
Seems much easier than to venture in and explore.
To look where emotions shrink, deep down inside.
Where the unconfident, insufficient and hesitant hide.
There lurks in my core, memories misunderstood.
Confused and contorted, from my childhood.
Reminding me of my weaknesses; anger and fear.
I must never complain, and do not dare shed a tear.

It masquerades as hunger, so I quell it with food,
But it rears up again with a vigour renewed.
I'm ashamed of my weight, and I'd love to be thin,
But I'm holding the extra weight of unworthiness within.

I try so hard to soothe it and keep it at bay.
The weight that I gain is the price that I pay,
For silencing a part of me that tries hard to be heard.
So I explore my inner feelings with the written word

Must I speak it out loud, so others bear witness to it?
If that exposes my weaknesses, then I am reluctant to do it.
Will I let fear rule my life then, and stay locked in my prison?
To 'stay safe' or 'enlighten', oh what an arduous decision.

I have built up an image that is perfect and polished.
To see the real me, must that be, demolished?
All my life I've worked hard to produce what you see,
The irony is it's just a reflection of me

A reflection is not real, there is no substance to it.
It has no thoughts or feelings, it can't perceive or intuit.
The real me is inside, just a tiny wee dot.
I've fooled myself for so long, that I almost forgot
That there is a real me, and I'm trying to be seen.
But I'm afraid of your judgement, please don't be mean.

Anger

An angry man behaves like a raging bull.
Issuing challenges with daring eyes,
He'll snort, lock horns and push or pull.
Hoping his opponents temper, will also rise.

He can lose control and come to blows.
He wants to cause pain at any cost.
With words or fists, as his anger grows.
Without anger, his argument would be lost

Who will back down first? The wiser man.
Who sees the situation for what it is.
He'll turn and walk away while he can.
Control and self-restraint are his.

Nothing can be gained when anger rules.
Emotion overtakes all reasoning.
Anger is an emotion reserved for fools,
Whose relationships it is poisoning.

Harsh Words

When there are harsh words that you need to say,
Don't try to take the coward's way.
Expressing anger is O.K.
Hold back and there's a price to pay.
Suppressed anger becomes amplified,
And deep inside you it will hide.
It causes imbalance in your mind,
So inner peace is hard to find.

A Travesty Of Justice

A travesty of justice, occurred this very day.
A man was found not guilty of his deeds in any way.
A child molester was acquitted of the deeds he was accused.
A little girl, her story bared is angry, and confused.

Her family also wonders why the charges didn't stick.
Is there justice in our country, or is the justice system sick?
Did magistrates and judges, and lawyers all conspire,
To let this guilty man go free and make the little girl a liar?

For five years she endured him and didn't dare to tell.
He told her he would kill her and kill her mum as well.
This man lived in her home and made her life a misery.
Till her mother caught him; but now you've set him free.

Shame on all of you who were supposed to put this man in jail.
How did justice not get served? How did the system fail?
What if suspected criminals could take a lie detector test?
Then all liars would be found guilty, and justice would cost less.

But what of all the lawyers, and magistrates and such?
The jurors and the judges, we wouldn't need them much.
What about the universities where they studied for so long,
To get qualified to do their jobs; ah maybe that's what's wrong.
This is a money making system designed to have no end,
We catch the bad guys then let them out so they can reoffend.

This keeps so many souls employed, you only need to look,
In Lonsdale Street at all the courts, no wonder things are crook.
Our economy could collapse if all lawmen were obsolete,
So little girls are sacrificed to keep big bucks in Lonsdale Street.

Australia- the lucky country? Well it is if you're a crim.
Talk to the man who was on trial, it's a lucky place for him.

Aussie farmer

I'm an Aussie farmer, and a poet as you see.
I live in natural beauty, I am healthy and I'm free.
But I do have one concern that disturbs my inner peace,
You think I'm cruel to animals, and you'd like for it to cease.

I understand your sentiment, farming does seem cruel at times.
But I work within the guidelines, I'm not committing any crimes.
I'm trying to make a living to feed my family as you do.
But I'm feeling a bit victimized, let me explain just why to you.

You set the price for produce by what you will or will not pay.
If you only buy the cheapest it's not fair of you to say,
We shouldn't keep our animals in such small spaces as we do.
We farm this way, so we can produce less expensive food for you.

You could put your money where your mouth is and pay a little more.
Buy the free range, not the battery eggs, when you go to the store.
Buy the grass fed, not the grain fed, it may be a little dearer.
Farmers supply what you can afford, does that make it any clearer.

If no-one bought the cheap stuff, that system would have to go.
You have the power to make or break us. I just thought you ought to know.
I don't like the system either and I believe it's time it changed.
Ethically produced food costs more but I'm sure it can be arranged.

Learning to fly

I've wanted to fly since I was three,
But my mother always cautioned me.
What goes up must come down, she always said,
And her words of wisdom have stayed in my head.
Still, every so often I'll give it a try,
You never can tell when you might fly.
The landings have always been hardest to master,
So far, they have all been a disaster.
Look at me now as I sail through the air,
Gliding by without a care.
I'll never stop trying,
Though it does really hurt,
Whenever I crash-land in the dirt.
The future will come, what will be will be,
The falls are hard, but I won't let that stop me.

Bushfire Advice

My whole world turned red and black smoke filled my eyes.
Fire roared in my ears, drowning the animal cries.
My farm was once beautiful but now it's scorched earth,
You can't tell to look at it, what it was once worth.

At least my family is safe, they left in the morning,
The strong wind and the heat were their early warning.
I thought I could stay and protect the sheds and our dwelling,
But there was no stopping that fire, and no way of telling,
If the fire truck could get here to give us a hand.
Foolish to hope, they were in such high demand.

It's lucky we built a fire bunker in case,
Of just such an occurrence; but it still was a race,
To reach it in time, behind the back shed.
If I'd waited another minute I'm sure I'd be dead

As it is I have burns to my hands and my face,
And the scars on my mind will be hard to erase.
I wouldn't do it again, it's just not worth the risk.
Possessions can be replaced, some things can't be fixed

Now I will never feel safe on a hot windy day.
If it were to happen again, there's no way I'd stay.
I've learned a valuable lesson through this ordeal.
To be a hero, for me, now holds no appeal.

We can't fight a fire when it gets to this size.
I thought I was strong, but I didn't realise.
How heat saps your strength, how your lungs burn with smoke.
How the noise of the fire instils fear in a bloke.
Next time I'll prepare and do what I'm told,
I will go with my family, and live to grow old.

Grandpa's Cases

Grandpa is a collector,
His favourite thing is cases.
He has so many of them,
That they won't stay in their places.
This morning when I was getting dressed,
While standing by the bed.
A case fell off the cupboard,
And hit me on the head.
I have to go to work now,
Though I am a little dazed.
You can be sure when grandpa gets home,
The matter will be raised.

New Secretary

Please get me a secretary who won't go away.
Who will sit in the office and do work all day.
Who doesn't have kids that might need her attention.
And never rushes off to a sales convention.
I'd prefer one who can spell, count and compute.
A sense of humour as well would be really beaut.
If she does dishes too then so much the better.
Where should I be looking, where can I get her?

I Wanted To Give You a Camel

I wanted to give you a camel,
And I finally got it caught.
It was the fastest one on earth,
And would be yours, or so I thought.
I spent a long time planning this,
I hoped it would make your day.
But when I went to wrap him up,
Your camel ran away.
You probably don't believe me,
And I wouldn't if I was you.
The only proof that he was ever here,
Is this bag of camel POO.

Trying To Learn Online

I struggle with learning online, but I am here right now.
I get that you are far away, and you can teach me how.
But I prefer to exist in the real world, not in cyberspace.
Couldn't we just do this lesson, in a classroom, face to face?

Am I old fashioned, that I prefer it this way?
It seems very complicated, to learn new things today.
Am I stuck in the past, or can I learn this new skill?
If I have an application for this, I know I can, and I will.
Convince me I need to do this, and I will certainly try.
But at the moment my most pressing question is why?

I know I'm supposed to keep up, and get with the times,
But I feel more comfortable at my desk writing rhymes.
I bow to your knowledge, although it seems kind of hazy.
Or maybe I'm not focussed,or my brain is too lazy,
To concentrate and take in what you are teaching.
We are so far apart,is this knowledge far reaching?

I can teach you about animals, and nature and stuff.
Because that's what I'm good at and, "I am enough".
But perhaps I could learn just a little bit more,
After all, that's what I am paying you for.

Is There a Role For The Aged Of Today?

I've just read a book called, "The "I" of the Beholder"
Written by a woman named Anne, who is older.

She has realized that though she is gifted and wise,
Her age makes her useless in society's eyes.
Is it sane that we throw away wisdom and learning?
When for understanding and wisdom we are all yearning.

Is there a role, for the aged of today?
A useful part in society, which they can play.
Although their mobility's reduced and their health has declined,
Does it follow that old people will all lose their mind?

What if their mind was perfectly sound?
Would we welcome them then?
Would we want them around?
They may be struggling with "future",
And be forgetting their past.
But what of the present
The present is vast.

To bring peace to the present,
Do we need all our senses?
If we loved enough,
Would it crumble defences?
How could we harness the essence of the aged?
Is there a task for them, that could keep them engaged?
If they could focus their thoughts on harmony and peace,
And forgive our past wrongs, would the bitterness cease?

To bring peace to the earth, we need a strong dose of love.
Could the elderly reach up, and pull it down from above.
And sprinkle it liberally on all who are near,
To help us overcome greed, anger and fear.

What if one day we could harness the power,
Of the minds of the aged,
And they could bloom like a flower.
And radiate love and peace like the sun,
Bringing harmony to the earth and joy to everyone.

My Dad (Eulogy)

My Dad was just an ordinary guy,
He didn't pretend to be anything more.
There was no pretence in him,
What you got was what you saw.
He wasn't always perfect,
But he did the best he could.
Most of us will remember him as gentle, kind and good.
He enjoyed sing-a-longs around the piano,
Religious discussions at the table.
Reciting poetry and sharing stories,
Whenever he was able.

Here is a story you may remember
That to me still seems so unreal.
Dad became a political activist,
To get the farmers a fair deal.
He organised a protest,
To gain attention to their plight,
By blockading the streets of Morwell
With heaps of tractors overnight.
The stunt got front page headlines,
Farmer Frank was a sensation.
Milk prices got some focus
In political conversations.

My Dad could change a tractor tyre,
And fix broken water pumps.
Mend machines with wire and hay band,
Shoot rabbits and pull up stumps.
He was often late for milking,
We had very patient cows.
He would drive to town to buy stockfeed,
It could sometimes take him hours.

My Uncle and Aunt came to visit once,
They were just chatting in the shed.
I'm not sure how it happened.
I don't know what was said.
But one minute my Aunt was standing there
In all her gorgeous clothes,
The next she was floundering in the trough
Why it happened "Dad only knows".

Sadly Dad sold the family farm when he and mum went separate ways.
We said goodbye to those patient cows, and the good 'ole farming days.
A short time later dad opened up, a new chapter in his life.
He met a girl called Nene, and took her for his wife.

He was the glue that bound together,
Many cousins and family friends.
He is the last of seven siblings,
This is where his generation ends.
The next generation will carry on
In the legacy of his love.
We know he will be with us
Looking down from up above.

Sometimes I'll catch a glimpse of him,
In the faces of my brothers
In the warm smiles of my sisters and their kind concern for others.
We're all sad to see you go dad,
But the memories will stay.
And our grandchildren will still hear of you,
Until OUR dying day.

Adventure

We're off on an adventure, our gear is packed and the weather is great.
We've looked forward to this moment for ages, now it's here and we just can't wait.
Before we head off there's instruction, about learning styles, goal setting and leading.
On a leadership camp it's important to learn, the people skills we will be needing.

The bus takes us up to the Snowies, and leaves us to carry our packs.
No problems so far we have plenty, of clothes, water and snacks.
We hike to the river well laden, and are elated to finally arrive.
Our packs were so heavy, the hills were so steep, we were happy to make it alive.

We're on our rafts in the water, we've been paddling now for four days.
Stopping for breaks in spectacular places, enjoying beauty wherever we gaze.
At nights we set up our bivvy,and cook up an odd sort of meal.
After a hard day paddling it's so welcome,tired but happy is how we all feel.

Often we're met with problems,and we do our best to overcome.
Wet bedding, blisters and sunburn are challenging for everyone.
We're off the river now and hiking, to a destination unknown.
We camp with the cows at a hayshed, that so much reminds me of home.

At night we experience caving, and come out bruised, exhausted and muddy.
We're so impressed with ourselves for having a go, and achieving tasks with our buddy.
Today we've been left in the bush to spend the night on our own.
To reflect on our journey and discover, what we have always known.
We're all capable of making the journey,but it's easier when not done alone.

My Grandparents Farm

It's hard to imagine they were once young.
And what the world was like when they'd just begun.
They cooked all their own food cos you couldn't just buy it,
And nobody needed to go on a diet.
Grandpas got furniture that he made by himself.
And he's made lots of nick-knack's that sit on the shelf.
There were no computers or iPads, back in those days.
They talked using smoke signals, that's what grandpa says.
I know he's kidding, I've seen old phones on TV.
Grandpa is always "taking the piss out of me"
That's what he calls joking, it's a strange expression.
Grandpa doesn't joke much, cos he's got depression.
That means he's grumpy and sleeps a fair bit.
And when he's awake he just likes to sit.
He likes to watch telly, he does it a lot,
You should see the piles of old movies he's got.
Grandma loves babies and animals and stuff,
She surrounds herself with them it seems she can't get enough.
At feed time it's so noisy you can't hear yourself think.
Maybe that's what drove my Grandpa to drink.
She locks them all safely in their pens over night,
Where they stay safe and warm until morning light.
Then she's back out there and at it again,
Feeding and cleaning her work has no end.
I like to help her when I come to stay.
I bottle feed baby goats and feed them some hay.
I love to sit with the rabbits, they make me feel calm.
There's always plenty to do on my Grandparents farm.

Our Washing Machine

Our washing machine is very old, it has served the family well.
I think it needs replacing though, do you know how I can tell.
The towels have lost their fluffiness, it's been transferred to our clothes.
Our whites are now a dirty brown, and where our socks are no-one knows.
The lids a little rusty, and the dials are hard to see.
But it's washed the clothes for thirty years, for five kids and Trev and me.

Workwear, school uniforms, footy gear and Sunday best.
It's worked hard for many years, to ensure we're cleanly dressed.
It deserves a medal for long service, and a grand retirement feast.
But retirement age has lifted now, five more years of work at least.

So if my clothes seem a little fluffy to you, when next we meet.
And my whites look dirty brown, or I have odd socks on my feet.
You'll understand the reason is, cos we've kept our old machine.
We've chosen long suffering and loyalty over keeping clean.

Traffic Slow? How's Your Blood Flow

As our city expands, and our population grows.
Our traffic increases, and as everyone knows.
Bottlenecks and traffic jams are bound to ensue.
Is there a way we can fix this? What should we do?

Imagine that roads are like arteries and veins.
That supply oxygen in blood to our organs and brains.
And our heart is like the city where business is done.
It pumps out goods and services to support everyone.
If our blood carried products we needed to survive,
We would patiently wait for the products to arrive.
But if our arterials weren't working, then our blood would stop flowing.
Can you see by this metaphor where I am going?
What happens in our bodies, also happens on our roads.
Neither function efficiently with unhealthy loads.

What happens in our veins when cholesterol's too high?
It can impede our blood flow, let's find out why.
It sticks to vein walls and builds up at the junctions,
Then the heart must work harder to fulfil all its functions.

It's just like the traffic jams we've been talking about,
Supplies take longer to get in, and more time to get out.
When the heart pumps the blood to the places it's needed,
Less energy's required if the flow is unimpeded.

Speaking of energy, now let's get back to our roads.
How much energy is wasted when the system overloads?
There are cars sitting idling while they wait to get going,
Stuck in the traffic because the roads are not flowing.

Exhaust fumes are polluting and drivers are stewing,
The roads are not working and a problem is brewing.
Research shows links between cholesterol and stress,
And stress shrinks our brain so we should do it less.

Commuters should be arriving at work refreshed and serene,
Instead they're late, and they're stressed, and they're craving caffeine.
Restriction in blood flow can cause an unstable mind,
A dangerous situation on our roads you will find.

A city functions more smoothly when commuters are early.
If they arrive late due to traffic, they can be taciturn and surly.
What can we do to improve the flow of our roads?
That can help reduce stress as we carry our loads?

Should we make the cars smaller,or make the roads wider,
Or create separate lanes for the motorbike rider.
What about pushbikes, trams, buses and trains?
We'll come up with an answer if we all use our brains.
As long as the blood flow is not being restricted,
And causing our minds to be confused and conflicted.

I wonder if we all took better care of our heart,
Our brains would work better and greater wisdom impart.
I wonder also if our cities became less congested,
Productivity would increase and we'd feel better rested.

For those who car pool and share a lift with a friend,
There's a fast lane on the freeway that I recommend.
If a fuel price reduction encouraged car pooling,
Perhaps it would make all of our journeys a little less gruelling.

What can we do to ease both types of congestion?
If you have an idea please let us hear your suggestion.
Many minds working together brainstorming this task,
Are more likely to find one, that's why we ask.

2017 International River Symposium

I went to the symposium to speak about water.
I'm passionate about it so I felt that I oughta.
There were delegates from countries far and wide.
I watched them all with feelings of pride.

With this many people sharing concerns and ideas,
We are on the right path although change can take years.
The 'welcome to country' was the best I've seen yet,
We partook in a ceremony I'll never forget.

Each presenter had 15 minutes to put forward their case,
They were many and varied but all in the right space.
Every presenter had such informative slides,
With data and graphs and words that were wise.

Their qualifications were impressive, and their job titles too,
But my brain started hurting before most were through.
I'm sure every presenter had at least one PhD,
They were all very clever, and then there was me..

Technologically challenged, but willing to try.
Not without reservations, I did ask myself ;why?
Why should these people listen to little old me,
What could I tell them that might help them see?

That the kids are the ones we should be trying to impress.
Facts and figures won't do it though, at least that is my guess.
Heart and emotion are the tools that we should be using,
To facilitate children's learning, that's what I am choosing.
When we are adults we are too hard to teach,
We try instead to convince others with our intellect and speech.
Our understanding is tainted by what we've been told,
Can our future be corrected then, by someone who's old?

We should teach children first to treat the land with respect,
To 'dress it and keep it' and all its creatures protect.
To force it to feed us is not the right way,
To plunder resources, at the end of the day,
Will cause us great harm because we don't understand,
How nature's processes have been symbiotically planned.
We cause an imbalance when we fail to see,
How everything is balanced so delicately.
When we disrupt one system there will be a domino effect,
Others systems will fail though they don't seem to connect.

Because we don't see the connections, doesn't mean they're not there.
To protect water we also need to protect the plants, soil and air.
When we have got that right the creatures will thrive,
And we'll be able to keep more animals and people alive.

I attended this conference to find those who have passion,
Who can teach what we need, each in his own fashion.
Those who believe water is a resource to share,
And are willing to protect it and treat it with care.
There were some who were wise in the ways of the land,
I will seek knowledge from them because they understand.
I am eager to listen, I am ready to learn,
And I will pass on the knowledge when it is my turn.

Another Perfect Day

I sit listening in silence, there is beauty all around.
The sound of flowing water, shapes and patterns on the ground.
Rocks of different colours, bugs on bended blades of grass.
The tweets and pips of little birds, I watch them as they pass.
Some spots of rain are falling, the air is damp and grey.
But I am not disturbed, as I enjoy another perfect day.

Cars and trucks are whizzing past somewhere in the distance,
The sound filters through my peaceful state and I offer no resistance.
I'm so grateful for the tranquillity, but I spare a fleeting thought,
For those who are not as fortunate, who in the web of life are caught.
Although peace is usually here, they will always pass it by.
Not knowing, and far too busy, and not as blessed as I

They have been at work all day, but I'm already home.
My garden is my haven, and I am in it all alone.
To find our perfect day, we don't really have to travel far.
It can be as close as our back door, there's no need to start the car.
If we sit quietly and listen, and breath deeply, we may find,
That tranquillity and peacefulness, are just a state of mind.

Arthur And Martha

Take a look at nature, and tell me if you can.
How a male frog becomes a female, and how a woman becomes a man.
Have we caused this problem, are we the ones to blame?
The sexes are homogenizing, they're all looking more the same.

There are chemicals in our water, that have run off from our crops
We used them to kill weeds, but their power never stops.
They run into our rivers and affect the fate of fish.
Will this affect us also, when it ends up on our dish?

Studies show chemicals affect many species, this we've seen.
But we keep spraying them on our crops, because it makes them lush and green.
Frog populations are decreasing because the sexes are confused.
The whole food chain is suffering because of the chemicals we've used.

It's a struggle telling Arthur from Martha in my world already.
The frogs are struggling cos they can't tell who is Freda, and who is Freddy
Fertility problems abound in many species on our earth.
That they are increasing is no secret, so here's my advice (for what its worth).

We need to stop and reassess; is what we're doing right?
Is there a way to do it better; can we reverse our plight?
It may be too late for us already, but we need to have a go.
Perhaps the answers are before us. If we don't look we'll never know.

Birds In Spring

From the comfort of my bed I can hear the birds awaking.
Through the misty morning sunrise flows the music they are making.
I can identify each bird in turn as it sings its morning greeting.
A cacophony of grateful sound ignites their morning meeting.

They're getting ready for their day; its spring, their chicks are hatching.
There's plenty of work for them to do, with parenting and bug-catching.
The adult birds fly back and forth, with mouths full to their nest.
To feed their chicks and keep them warm, there is no time for rest.

Springtime is the time of year when everything is growing.
Grass and trees are clean and new and creeks are overflowing.
Baby birds of all types abound, and everything is green.
Sun and white clouds fill the sky, there's no grey to be seen.

Spring is the time to celebrate, to make loud and joyous sounds.
For all nature to reawaken, and shake off its winter frowns.
Vibrations pulsate through the air and stir everything to action.
But I snuggle back into my cosy bed with grateful satisfaction.

How To Explain Rain

Precipitation falls as rain.
Evaporation takes it up again.
Percolation doesn't make a sound,
As the rain quietly seeps into the ground.
Transpiration occurs through grass and leaves,
This is the water vapour that a cloud receives.
Condensation is the process where,
Water vapour, high up in the air,
Become drops that fall as rain.
Then the cycle
Starts
Again.

Farming With Nature

There's much more to the water cycle than first meets the eye.
We know it rises from the ground, and see it falling from the sky.
The oxygen cycle greatly depends, on grasses plants and trees.
Which exchange CO_2 for oxygen with such apparent ease.

Nutrient cycles careful intertwine with water, soil, and air.
Earths efficient natural systems, are made with deliberate care.
Did you ever stop to wonder, what makes it work this way?
How all things work together? Will we understand some day?
I ponder on the process, because I find it helps me grow.
And I would love to share with all of you, the little that I know.

Where the rain falls often, there is a prevalence of life.
Where there is a lack of rain, plant scarcity is rife.
And yet some creatures still survive, they adapt to drought conditions.
What they struggle to survive with though, is the chemical additions.

When rain falls on crops, that have agricultural sprays.
It washes from the farmland, into our waterways.
Some soaks into the soil, and is taken up by plants.
Then becomes part of our food chain, and continues to advance.

They may be ingested by an animal, and then in turn by us.
We didn't realise this would happen, and we don't make a fuss.
But the consequences of this, affects our quality of life.
Disease becomes the norm; our health systems are in strife.

When old or sick plants die, they are absorbed back into the soil.
Where microscopic creatures are affected as they toil.
Each tiny creature has a function, even those that we can't see.
They are all playing an important role in the soils fertility.

Some break down the carbon, while others gobble waste.
Symbiotically they function, all their actions interlaced.
When we affect the balance with our agricultural sprays,
Our soil fertility is compromised in very many ways.

To farm healthy crops, we need certain nutrients to do it.
We doubt the soils fertility, and so we add them to it.
But we don't need to do that if we treat our soil well.
If we were more aligned with nature, the benefits would tell.

What we're doing currently, because we think that we know best,
By "enhancing" nature's productivity, has put her to the test.
We've disrupted the fine balance, and created plants that can't survive.
Without pesticides and fungicides, to help them stay alive.

Some insect's roles are to get rid of any plants that might be sick,
If more of them are needed, they can multiply real quick.
Since our crops are often compromised with artificial feed,
We have to kill the insects off, so we put poison on the seed.

Not everything that creeps or crawls is by definition a pest.
The creatures that live within the soil give it fertility and zest.
There are several soil nutrients that healthy crops require.
To obtain the quality of crops to which all farmers may aspire.

Let's look at some soil nutrients, and find out how they're made.
We'll need a microscope to see, and to dig we'll need a spade.
Nitrogen is found on root nodules, in every legume crop.
It's also in manure, which animals generously spread on top.

Legumes are plants that convert nitrogen, from gas out of the air,
Into a usable form in the dirt, so other plants can access it there.
Micro-organisms in the soil are part of this process too.
As are worms and other bugs, and even lightning, but who knew.

As plants grow old and die, they become a nutrient reservoir.
And hold moisture in the soil, on which other plants can draw.
Potassium is important, the "quality nutrient" as it's known.
It affects the size, colour, and taste of all food plants that are grown.

It can be found in compost, wood ash, and decomposing fruit.
There'll be slow and stunted growth, if a soil deficiency is acute.
Phosphorous and sulphur are two elements that are found,
When weathered rocks release them both, from deep within the ground.

Phosphorous helps with energy storage, healthy bones and teeth.
Sulphur helps fix nitrogen in root nodules, in the soil beneath.
There are so many different nutrients, that work together in this way.
Each as important as the next. Nature's laws we should obey

Nature has already put fertilizing components, into the soil and air.
We won't need to add any extra, if we farm diligently and with care.
In fact if we do, we may cause accidental harm.
Causing death to plants and animals, while spreading poison on the farm.

Some forms of sulphur and nitrogen, although easy to obtain,
When used as chemical fertilizers can return as acid rain.
Acid rain causes death and destruction to both animals and plants,
And to insect workers in the soil, like dung beetles, worms and ants.

Crop rotation, animal grazing, and letting paddocks rest.
Is how we should keep soil balanced; nature does know best.
We've farmed this way before, for many past hundreds of years.
But when we interfere and force the land, its fertility disappears.

If we don't respect the soil and we keep trying to farm intensively,
We will disrupt all the natural systems, and damage soil extensively.
To help our earth to do its job, we must continually strive,
To work more cooperatively with nature, if we all want to survive.

From My Kitchen Window

From my kitchen window, I watch the seasons change.
As nature does its work, I see my garden rearrange.
In autumn falling leaves, turn orange red and brown.
Children gaily roll among them, as they heap upon the ground.

Gusts of winter wind blow in, decorating trees in frost and ice.
Orb Weaver webs, outlined by frost, invite me to look twice.
The orange tree produces flowers that stay until the spring.
A promise of the tasty treat that this sweet fruit will bring.
Wattle trees start to flower, when the winter's nearly over.
And daffodils and other bulbs rise up through the clover.

As spring warms the ground, the garden grows, blossoming with new life.
Birds swoop and dart amongst the plants, chasing insects, which are rife.
New leaves unfurl to clothe naked trees; nests in branches can be seen.
The cold still greyness of winter morphs into a fresh and vibrant green.

Summer comes with scorching heat, causing plants to wilt and wither.
Storms arrive with thunder claps, bringing precious water; the life giver.
The North wind dries the garden, Ferntree fronds hang limply down.
From springs fiddleheads so fresh and new, to a dried up crunchy brown.

Autumn greens the lawn and vegie patch, we harvest what we've sown.
The plants enjoy the milder weather, see how much they all have grown.
Mushrooms appear in the lawn and toadstools pop-up under trees.
The grandkids blow on dandelions and chase fairies in the breeze.
Apples, pears, and other fruit, are not yet ripe to pick.
Cheeky parrots are tasting them, so we must cover them up quick.
The cycles of the seasons, I watch through my window from year to year.
As they work their magic in my garden, I feel so blessed to live right here

Nothing We Can Do

We thought they were well suited, they seemed so perfectly matched.
They looked so comfortable together, almost like they were attached.
He is broken hearted, he knows he's caused her misery.
But he felt something wasn't right, and he needed to be free.
I'm sorry he hurt her feelings, I know that she is suffering too.
As mothers we can feel their pain, but there's nothing we can do.

His heart is broken his heads messed, up he has so many fears.
How long will he be like this, for weeks or months or years?
I hope someday she can forgive him, my heart aches for her too.
As mothers we can feel their pain, but what else can we do?

We can comfort them and listen, when they tell us they are sad.
We can hug them and console them, when we know they're feeling bad.
We don't get to make their choices, they have to do that on their own.
We could when they were children, but not now that they are grown.
Choices of forever, like commitment to one spouse.
To buy a car, to have a child, or to live together in one house.
Are theirs to make and theirs alone, and though we're desperate to,
As mothers we can't tell them; it's something they should do.

For some, choices are hard because they struggle with indecision.
They feel suffocated by it; by the risk. They like precision.
They need to know how it turns out, before they can commit.
But the future is uncertain, we can guess but we can't know it.
Perfectionists don't make mistakes, they procrastinate instead.
They are most cautious in their nature, fear of failure fills their head.
As mothers we may know all this, we may have been in that place too.
And though we may want to fix it, there's nothing we can do.

This poem is actually about my business which was like a child to me.

Moving On

My youngest child is leaving home, at least that's how it feels to me.
I gave him all I had to give, now I have to set him free.
We shared our lives for 20 years; now this part of our journey ends.
Precious memories kept close forever, remind me, we were best friends.

My world revolved around him, everything I did was for his good.
If I could only turn back time, you know I very nearly would.
But then our lives would stagnate, our relationship would be unfulfilling.
For him to grow, this I know, to let him move on I must be willing.

I wish him well, as he moves into the next phase of his existence.
And I'll let him go with dignity, and offer no resistance.
Nothing in this life stays the same, and so change I must embrace.
Although losing him is hard to bear, I'll do it with ease and grace.
When I look back, I'll remember him just as he used to be.
He was everything I needed, a gift sent just for me.

How Does Water Get To The Mountains?

How does water get to the mountains, since they are higher than the seas?
If gravity makes all water run down, how does water get up to the trees?
Do trees store water inside their trunk, how do they get it in there?
How does it get from their roots to their leaves, and what happens when they are bare?

There are answers to all these questions and it's important that we all know.
That for trees to survive they need water and food, just like us, In order to grow.
Trees are a most important part of the land, they help spread the water around.
If it wasn't for trees, there would be much less rain, in our waterways and in the ground.

Trees are like pumps they suck water up, through narrow tubes, a bit like our veins.
They take water from within the ground, which is replenished whenever it rains.
How do they do this you might ask, when gravity makes all things go south.
Well the roots of the trees which are down in the soil, are very much like the trees mouth.

They suck up the water, through their specialised tubes, that's how all the trees eat.
It seems to me that they are upside down, their mouths are down at their feet.
The water carries within it nourishment, that travels to all the trees different parts.
Their tubes connect from the roots to the leaves, and that's where the real magic starts.

Each of the leaves has little holes called stomata, through which transpiration occurs.
Negative pressure develops inside the leaf, when the vapour to the air transfers.
This causes suction throughout the tree, from the leaves right down to the roots.
It works like a pump to lift water, one of the trees many great attributes.

When water transpires from the leaves, and evaporates into clouds in the sky.
The wind blows them further inland, like a huge mobile water supply.
As the millions of tons of water, in the form of tiny droplets, get bigger.
Precipitation occurs, causing rain to fall to the earth with great vigour.

Precipitation is just a fancy word used to describe the process of rain.
Which starts as water sucked up by a tree, and transpires to the clouds again.
Now what would happen if the trees were removed, especially those near the coast.
Water couldn't move inland anymore, all trees matter, but these do the most.

To remove these trees from the cycle is like taking the inlet pipe from the tank.
If you are trying to pump water from it, I'm afraid you'll be drawing a blank.
The trees near the coast are critical, to help pump water further inland.
Evaporation takes their vapour up to the clouds, as I'm sure you by now understand.

The clouds are then blown along by the wind, carrying all the water stored there.
To release it onto the plains or the hills, showering it down through the air.
For the rain to reach to the countries centre, there must be trees all along the way.
If there are no big trees left don't worry, grasses and scrub are O.K.

As long as there's some sort of vegetation, to hold all the soil in place.
The rain will be gratefully received, and some vapour will go back into space.
Up into the clouds again, to be blown further along by the breeze.
Nature has designed this system, to move water up hills with ease.

Many things contribute to our weather, but if there are not enough trees about.
The water cycle will be broken, and the area will be plunged into drought.
What can we do for our country, to make sure the water cycle keeps going?
Plant more trees everywhere, if you really care; it's the trees that keep water flowing.

The Earth Is Like A Turtle

The scutes on a turtle, have individual names.
Each scute is growing larger, and that is what explains.
Why the shell never gets too small to fit the turtle in it.
His carapace and plastron protect his body every minute.

He can't wander off and sunbake, outside of his shell.
Cos it's attached onto his bones, it's his skeleton as well.
His shell is like a rib cage, it's a special type of bone.
It keeps him safe from predators, it also is his home.

Our Earth is like a turtle shell, tectonic plates are like the scutes.
The Earth's enlarging all the time, (about this there were disputes).
That tectonic plates keep growing, is our new understanding.
Like when you blow up a balloon it's stretching and expanding.

Our earth was once a third the size, it was a ball of mostly land.
Cracks appeared and oceans formed, and it started to expand.
Fissures were caused by trembling, deep within earth's core.
Larva flowed up through them, expanding earth's crust a little more.

As each tectonic plate grew, countries that were once near,
Grew ever distant over time and more water filled our sphere.
Where did the water come from, if it wasn't there before?
Let's look far below earth's surface, in order to explore.

A thousand K's beneath the crust, where Earth's pressure is increased.
Rocks called Ringwoodite store water, three oceans worth at least.
When the internal pressure builds up, earth tremors can ensue.
Water is released and, with molten lava gushes through,
Cracks between tectonic plates, where it explodes into the air
As superheated gas and steam, splattering lava everywhere.

The Earth when it was born, stored most of its water deep within.
Now the oceans form two thirds of the entire earth's outer skin.
How did this change occur, when did the earth become so wet?
Water's been stored deep down in rocks, within earth's mantle don't forget.

At some time during earth's development, a great flood event occurred,
And water poured forth from the deep as history has concurred.
You may have heard of Noah's ark, and dismissed it as a fable.
Scientists though now agree there is enough evidence on the table,
To support the "great flood theory", there are fish fossils on the mountains.
In Noah's story as it was told, "the deep erupted into fountains".

Now just to re-cap on this, so you're less likely to forget,
How the earth is like a turtle, (for those who haven't got it yet).
Every now and then,when we feel a rumble or a shaking.
That's earth's pressure building; it can make the ground start quaking.
Tectonic plates are shifting and colliding, and expanding along their seam.
Creating gaps in the ocean floor, through which comes molten lava, gas and steam.

Lava cools and new land forms, in the cracks through which it came.
Like a turtle whose scutes are growing, the process is the same.
Nature is full of fractals, of that I am quite sure.
To understand our planet better, I just look around for more.

"As above so below", explains our reality quite clearly.
Many mysteries can be solved if we investigate sincerely.
To discover hidden secrets, if that's your passion or your aim.
Take a closer look in nature, at what is different, but the same.

If I Was A Tree

If I was to compare myself to a tree,
Here are some similarities you would see.
Tree leaves are like lungs, they filter the air.
They take out impurities that may be in there.
We need water to drink, it goes in through our mouth.
Their water comes from a bit further south.
They draw water up through their roots, from the ground.
Did you know that water moving in trees makes a sound?

My stomach is like the soil, its job is to digest.
It turns carbon into food, which gives me my zest.
My gut flora work like the insects in the soil.
They each do their job, how busily they toil.
To send nutrients to my blood, my life to sustain.
My blood's like the tree's sap, but where's the tree's brain?

I know trees can communicate through the air with each other.
And they can receive nourishment through the roots of another.
They warn each other, when an herbivore's approaching.
How can they do this without any visible coaching?
I'd very much like to know how this is achieved.
Before I read about trees, I would not have believed
That they have thoughts and emotions, and feel pain too.
They have families and communities as well. But who knew?
They're just like me! Oh how nature amazes.
The more I learn about nature, the more questions it raises.
How dependant we are on all that's around.
In the air, the water, and especially the ground.

Lake Without A Name

I live above a lake.
A lake without a name.
It has no water in it,
But is spectacular all the same.
It's not there every day,
It comes and goes at will.
On frosty winter mornings,
When the air is very still,
It appears as if by magic.
It just happens over night.
When I look out in the morning,
I am so grateful for this sight.
I drink in the splendour while I can.
Cos I know when the sun climbs high,
My lake will disappear again,
Into the clear blue sky.

Letting Nature Be Our Guide

When our mind is full of facts, and our head is in the cloud.
And the practicalities of life,seem to not have been endowed.
When we think we know the answer, but in fact have no idea.
We become as one unteachable, as though our ears don't hear.

When we listen to our gut,which interprets data from our senses.
Intuition and understanding, are the natural consequences.
But this ability seems to leave us,when we educate our mind.
We lose the tap that turns it on, we might look but may not find.

The way to turn it on again, involves swallowing our pride
And accepting we have fallen short, and to let nature be our guide.
Nature will not let us down if we watch and learn her ways.
To work in harmony with her laws, will produce results that will amaze.

She is a gentle teacher and can wait for us to reach the stage,
Where we stop trying to prove ourselves and humbly turn the page.
To begin writing a new chapter, one where we both work together.
Where we can live in harmony, from that day forward to forever.

Teaching Children About Nature

Our children are precious, so is the earth.
How should we teach them, how much it is worth?
They'll make decisions that affect the future of our nation.
They may usher in world peace, and see earth's regeneration.

How should we lead them, in the way they should go?
Can we help them, to learn all they need to know?
Children's brains are receptive, they can take in far more,
Than most of us adults give them credit for.

Let them see nature, let them touch it and feel it.
Nature will teach them, let's not try to conceal it.
Don't pollute their minds with tables, graphs and data.
To learn through experience, will help them to be smarter.

With our technical talk we put knowledge in their head.
We need to let them feel nature in their hearts more instead.
They can learn wisdom through observation and action.
Our obsessive need for more data can become a distraction.

It can deviate us from what we are trying to achieve.
I look at your infographics and find it hard to believe.
That you have a feel for the problem and will find a solution,
Because we are the problem, we are the pollution.

Put your computers away and go down to the rivers,
Sit and talk for a while with nature's life givers.
Notice what happens when the river flows fast,
And how tranquillity comes when it slows down at last.

Our minds are like this, they need peacefulness too.
To let the river of thoughts and emotions flow through.
Listen and learn, let understanding flow in.
It can't happen when there's too much input (data and din).

That's a type of pollution called clutter of mind.
Like pollution of river, it leaves a huge mess behind.
Pollution of body is like pollution of land.
If we load food with chemicals it can get out of hand.

Then we go to the doctor when we feel sick,
And he gives us a pill, which should heal us real quick.
But instead it reacts with the last pill we took.
It's no wonder we all, so often feel crook.

When our soil has a problem, we try a chemical solution,
Unaware that we are really compounding soil pollution.
Our understanding is tainted by what we've been told,
Can systems in nature be understood, by someone who is old?

Once we become adults I think we become too hard to teach.
We become set in our ways, our thoughts, and our speech.
We need a new approach from young, and unpolluted minds.
Let's wait and see what solutions, the next generation finds.

The Journey Of Water

Grey clouds in the sky are heavy with rain.
It falls to the earth on thirsty terrain.
Some falls in the forest, some falls on the field.
The plants are all grateful and increase their yield.
Rivulets form and run down into creeks,
From forests that flourish on ranges and peaks.
Soil creatures rejoice, all nature gives thanks,
Reservoirs fill as do lakes, dams and tanks.
Puddles are many and frogs lay their eggs.
Toddlers in gumboots splash rain up their legs.
Umbrellas pop up to keep our clothes dry,
But our water's in crisis. Let me explain why.

Our great forests are felled, some ranges lay bare.
There's nothing to hold the soaking rain there.
The soil can't absorb it, there's no humus left,
A vital component of which it's bereft.
It rushes in torrents down the hillside,
And gauges scars in the land in its wild downhill ride.
To the creeks and rivers the rainwater goes tumbling,
It's barely contained, river banks start crumbling.
Gone are the tree roots that once held them in place,
Angry and turgid the flood picks up pace.
I'm sure you can guess what the outcome will be.
What makes this happen? Read on and you'll see

Our disappearing forests are the lungs of the earth.
They prevent climate change, but now there's a dearth,
We can expect more floods, fires and weather events,
Increased temperatures and droughts. A bleak future presents.

Now let's go back in our journey to where rain fell on farms,
On crops and on pasture on livestock and barns.
What changes occurred there that should cause concern?
Let's investigate thoroughly so we can learn.

On the journey through farmland many poisons were met,
On the leaves, grass and soil, and once they were wet,
The poisons washed into the water and ran
Into the waterways of the cities of man.
Chemicals in farming have some "time saving" features,
But they're toxic to microbial life and soil creatures.
Are farmers to blame for this state of affairs?
In the case of pollution is the fault solely theirs?

Let's look at our contribution, though to us it seems small,
Water is piped to our houses and is accessible to all.
As long as water comes out when we turn on the tap
We don't care to know more or to look at a map,
To see the journey of water and how it got there,
We live in the city, why should we care?

We bathe in it, wash with it and do all our cleaning.
Our plants and our lawns with grey water are greening.
Our cleaning compounds and chemical "stuff"
Gurgle down plug holes, it seems we can't get enough.
Adverts promised more clean for less effort, in less time as well
So we have more free time, but what didn't they tell?

In our quest for more time and cleaning with ease,
Was it mentioned that pollution causes disease.
As our wash water disappears down the drain,
Do we remember that it was once rain?
Would we drink it now, I doubt we would dare,
But fish in the creek do when it ends up there.
They haven't much choice, nor do the frogs
As they struggle to survive in the swamps and the bogs.
It's easy to point and blame pollution on others,
But we are in this together we are all brothers.
Soil creatures, livestock, fish, frogs and us,
All suffer together, now let us discuss.

Are our dilemmas caused by nature or man, you decide.
Could we manage land better, who'll be our guide?
Politics, economics, convenience, science?
To live in harmony with nature we must form an alliance.
A stronger connection is what we all need,
Connection with nature, disconnection from greed.

Let us start with the air the water and ground.
What things can **we do** to turn all this around?

The Oceans Are Rising

(Child)
The oceans are rising. How long will it be?
Before the lowlands are swallowed up by the sea
How many cities do you think will go under?
How will global warming affect us, I wonder?

Both Poles are melting more by the minute,
The sea will soon have no icebergs left in it.
The glaciers are calving and falling apart.
How can we fix this? Where should we start?
Does this mean in winter there'll be no more snow?
How did this happen, because I want to know?

(Grandma)
Our world is changing of this there's no doubt,
How to stop it is what everyone's talking about.
Pollution's a huge problem, and we are all to blame.
Working together to fix it should be our aim.

The problems all started way back in the past.
It started off slowly then grew exponentially fast.
As the population increased and industry grew,
Pollution began, but nobody knew.

Factories belched toxic smoke into the air,
But the businesses prospered, they didn't care.
When cars were invented, as everyone knows,
Oil and petrol were needed, so we dug wells for those.

We mined minerals from soil and built houses from wood.
We sprayed chemicals on our crops because "good farmers should".
With every generation pollution grew worse.
We've plundered our planet. Mankind is a curse.

By the time we noticed what we'd done to the world,
We could only look on in horror as disaster unfurled.
I believe that our problems all started with greed.
Humans always seem to want more than they need.

Maybe your generation can come up with a solution,
To end this consequence of greed, which we call pollution.
I don't think you could do worse than we did in our day.
What are your thoughts, what do you have to say?

(Child)
Well if the problem is caused in part by bad air,
Can't we fix it by planting lots of trees everywhere?
Trees breath in bad air and breath fresh air back out,
In school this is what we've been learning about.

(Grandma)

Perhaps, but there's something trees can't live without.
Something that there isn't much of in a drought.
They'll need lots of water to help them to grow,
And when they're big they'll drink water from deep down below.
Strange as it seems this can help create rain,
As it evaporates from the leaves and falls down again.

(Child)

But if that's the solution then hadn't we oughta,
Start planting right now while we still have some water.
And could we make it illegal to cut any trees down,
Could we plant more in every piece of useable ground?

(Grandma)

You're right of course, no piece of ground should be bare,
Exposure to sunlight kills micro-organisms in there.
It also means topsoil can blow away in the breeze,
Roots bind it together; Roots of grass and of trees.

To plant trees is great, but sometimes grasses are better.
Grass roots and soil organisms can all work together.
They filter the air also, and remove toxic gas.
The roots of long grasses have a much greater mass,
For the storage of carbon, and when the grass dies,
Micro-organisms feed on it and here's a surprise;

Animals are an important part of this grass cycle too,
For soil creatures to stay healthy, they need animal poo.
If we let animals graze and plant more, shrubs, trees, and grass,
It may help this problem to eventually pass.

(Child)
Then let's get to work, there's no time to waste.
Before our water runs dry, we'd better make haste.
Grandma do you think this will work, it's my only Idea,
I can think of no other to make our air nice and clear.

(Grandma)
We can't turn back time we can only move forward
This is a great solution to be working toward

(Child)
We can't tell if it will work till we give it a go
It just might improve things. **We** both hope so!

The Role Of Insects

Plants live and die in the forests and fields, and eventually return to the soil.
How does this happen you may ask. Watch the insects as they busily toil.
Have you noticed that wherever you go, the insects are already there?
In the trees, the ground our gardens and homes, nits can even live in our hair.
Insects are the most dominant creatures on earth, and we always thought it was us.
We kill them with whatever means we can, but there's something we need to discuss.

What would the world be like, if with our poisons, we made all insects dead?
What food then would the spiders eat? They might have to eat us instead.
Insects are food for spiders and birds, and for millions of other little creatures.
But that's not the best thing about them, we don't see their most useful features.

Bugs make the soil in which plants grow, when plants die, we call it decay.
Have a close look when you see a dead tree, how does it end up that way?
Describe what you see when you look inside, where the tree appears rotten and hollow.
Somehow it seems that dirt has got in, so have insects, and spiders will soon follow.
An army of ants is crawling around, each industriously carrying its load.
They're taking supplies back to their colony, in their deep underground abode.

Cockroaches are busily chewing, and pooing, and turning the wood into dirt.
It is an amazing thing to observe the tree, and see it slowly but steadily convert.
Millions of insects are working, to create soil that is full of good stuff.
Producing fertile soil on which all life depends, we really can't thank them enough.

Over time all plants will grow old die, and it's just as well that we've got,
Such industrious creatures so willing to help, and luckily there are a lot.
So next time you reach for insecticide, remember the part that they play,
And look instead to see what you can do, to encourage the insects to stay.

Tumbles The Wombat

Tumbles was a wombat, he lived inside by the fire.
In a bag inside a box, with a lid of wood and wire.
He wasn't very big, but he had lots of strength.
To escape his box to find me, he would go to any length.

One night while I was sleeping, he walked up to my bed.
"You should be sleeping Tumbles, I'll put you back", I said
Later I heard an unusual sound, so I sat up in bed and saw,
A naughty little wombat, scratching noisily at my door.

This time when I put him back, I put a heavy log on the lid.
That should keep him in I thought, as between the sheets I slid.
Never underestimate a wombat, they're determined and they're strong.
The extra weight had slowed him down, but not for very long

Before I even got to sleep I heard the pitter- patter of little claws,
As he scampered down the passage, to the tune of Trevor's snores.
I tied him inside his bag this time, and gently put him back.
"That will keep him in" I said, as I climbed back in the sack.

How wrong was I, he missed me so, and though it took a while.
He, in his bag, rolled through the door and I just had to smile.
If the little fella's so determined to sleep in my bed tonight,
How could I refuse him, I think he had earned the right.

We Didn't Know

I have a question I'd like answered, but I'm not sure who to ask.
So I'll talk to anyone I can, because I feel it is my task.
There's a problem in our water, caused by the way our soil is used.
Too many chemicals are poured on, it's being chemically abused.
Can we change the way we farm, so that we don't cause disease?
Can we align ourselves with nature, and work alongside it please?

If we keep farming practices as they are, it won't be very long.
Before our soil won't produce any crops, 'cos we're doing it all wrong.
Not only are we poisoning the soil, in which we grow our food.
There is "runoff" to our lakes; chemical cocktails are being brewed.

Our water is not fit to drink, in so many areas already.
Nature's perfect balance has now become quite unsteady.
Did we really think we could improve on what nature has provided.
Have we become so brainwashed that our focus is divided.
We are being hoodwinked, into believing nature needs a hand.
Now look what we have done to the productivity of our land.

We've travelled so far down the wrong path, I don't know if we'll get back.
There's really no alternative now, so we'll just have to "have a crack".
If we keep having children, there'll soon be nowhere for them to live.
The crops will fail, because our impoverished soil, has nothing more to give.

They may need to become nomads in the hope of finding where,
The ground produces a little food, and they can stop and settle there.
Their futures looking pretty bleak, I only wish that it weren't so.
I hope they can forgive us because, "we really didn't know".

What Is Soil Made Of?

My body waste, though repulsive to me,
Can be made into delicious food for a tree.
How does this happen? How can it be?
There is life in the soil, look close and you'll see.
Manure is a "treat" with many good features,
Prized highly by worms and other soil creatures.
They digest this goodness and before very long,
It becomes part of the soil that keeps our trees strong.

What other things in the soil can be found?
Let's get a magnifying glass and take a good look around.
Fungi and roots help hold the soil together.
So it can't get washed, or blown away, in bad weather.
Decaying leaves hold the water that trees need to drink,
They make the soil like a sponge, amazing don't you think?

Have a look at the creatures that live in the soil,
They all play their part and busily toil,
To convert dirt into food for trees, grass and plants.
There are beetles and spiders, worms, crickets, and ants,
And so many others you've only to look
In your own back yard, no need to search in a book.

While small creatures busily devour unimaginable things,
The soil grows more fertile and up green life springs.
All life depends on our soil, so when you next need to 'go',
Think of those hungry soil creatures waiting patiently below.

White Faced Heron

There is a white faced heron that has moved into our backyard.
It's not easy to see her nest, although to hear her is not hard.
The squawk she makes is very loud, but melodious it's not.
She loudly trumpets her ascent, as she flies up to her spot.
Her legs and neck and beak are long, her wingspan is quite wide.
She seems to breastroke through the air, rather than to glide.
Her long legs keep her plumage dry, as she wades in swamps and marshes.
With her long and pointed beak she digs for worms in reeds and grasses.
I hope her eggs all hatch this year but only time will tell.
It will be nice if she returns next year and brings her young as well.

Our bird population drifts back and forth,
it has changed throughout the years.
Once Kookaburras laughed and Magpies warbled, now new sounds fill our ears.
Bell birds "tink" like tiny bells and King Parrots fly, unafraid into our view.
Young galahs squawk all summer long,
giving their mum plenty of work to do.
What causes the population shift?
Is it the food source that is changing?
Are there less worms and bugs now for the birds? Are their niches rearranging?
I know that birds have territories but what makes them disappear,
When they have lived in one location, quite content, year after year?
What change occurs in their territory that in some way explains,
What has become their hardship from which another species gains?
Does the food source most available change from insects into seeds,
Requiring one family to look further afield in order to fulfil their needs?
While another type moves in to take advantage, of whatever is aplenty.
So where there once was one pair, it seems there now are twenty.
What is occurring in the landscape to bring about this change?
What is causing the bird populations to slowly but surely rearrange?

Nature never stays the same, small changes frequently occur.
Evolution marches on regardless of what we think we would prefer.

Save Our Farmers

I grew up on a dairy farm where I helped to milk the cows.
Our shed was rather antiquated so milking would take hours.
When 'Herringbones' were all the rage, each of our neighbours in succession,
Upgraded to the more modern style, but dad said "after the depression".

To say the economy was depressed then was actually not quite true,
It was dad who sometimes suffered; but he could get excited too.
I thought him such a clever man, there wasn't much he didn't know,
He would often dream up strange ideas and give a few of them a go.

He came up with a plan to help his fellow farmers end the plight,
Of cripplingly low milk prices. He inspired some of them to fight.
A tractor blockade was formed and all the farmers drove to town,
It made the news and brought attention to milk prices going down.

Fair prices are still a problem though and still the farmers strive,
To feed their families on a pittance and keep their businesses alive.
Generations of farmers come and go but few now stay on the land,
Their work is hard and dirty, and they often need the bank to lend a hand.

To be a farmer in the old days required knowledge and intuition,
To know which pastures needed rest, and how to provide the right nutrition.
To understand their animals needs, they would get to know each cow.
But not everything they did back then was done the way we would do it now.

Clearing land and draining swamps was done without much thought,
Ploughing slopes that were too steep created paddocks that were fraught,
With ground instability, loss of soil, and sediment in the creeks.
Not to mention the erosion that occurred on slopes and peaks.

Mistakes were made back then of course, and from some we learned a lot.
But we should look back more often because I think maybe we forgot,
That animals provide our income and of them we should take good care.
Intensive farming provides cheaper meat but buyers please beware.

The price that is paid for produce that is produced on farming land,
Has been pushed down to the limit although there is such a high demand.
The big produce buyers have reduced it, so they can make more money.
And pass some savings on to us, the consumer, but here's what's funny;

The more we save by buying cheap, the unhappier we become,
Because the cheaper food that's mass produced is poisoning everyone.
The poisons not only in our fruit and vegies, but it's in our meat as well.
And while intensively farmed animals are cheaper, they have to live in hell.

At least back in the old days, a farmer cared for his stock and land.
Now money talks much louder, and as consumers we should understand.
We drive the market with our dollars, by what we are willing to pay,
This dictates how our food's produced. Should it be this way?

And even though we know this, we still choose dollars over sense.
How can we put all the blame on farmers for this capital offense?
We all contribute to the problem by not paying what foods worth.
We should learn to grow food ourselves, and take good care of the earth.

When times are tough, in droughts and floods, or when prices take a dive.
The farmer keeps on growing our food, he has to, to survive.
Where would we be without him or her? Could we learn to grow our own?
We have become so far removed, would we know how seeds are sown?

The skills that farmers have retained, have taken generations to acquire.
And as more farmers leave the land, the situation becomes more dire.
Who is going to feed us city folk, when all the farmers leave their farms?
They're all moving into the suburbs, this should be setting off alarms.

Eighty percent of the world's population already lives in a city,
If more farmers walk off their land the outcome won't be pretty.
The knowledge loss of how to grow our food is going to be alarming,
If we don't do something now, to halt this haemorrhage from farming.

Giving And Receiving

In this life there are two pleasures, they are giving and receiving.
But when receiving becomes taking it's very much like thieving.
I dearly love to give, but I hate when I feel used.
It makes me feel upset when my generosity is abused.

So then what makes a person give even when he knows,
That his gifts hold little value, to the receiver, of those?
Do we give to be liked, or do we give to be accepted?
Do we give 'cos we want to, or because giving is expected?

Does resentment build up, when the sentiment's not returned?
Is our self-worth deflated, a bit like one whose love is spurned?
What things can we do to encourage reciprocal giving?
Because it's then that I think we'll start symbiotic living.

Our human nature is visible in how we treat the earth.
We expect it to produce, but we don't pay what it is worth.
We take what we want and forget to give it some return.
We could observe the animals, but I wonder if we'd learn.

Animals and plants have mutualism down to a fine art.
Each one has a job to do and they all play their part.
Living together in harmony, appears not so hard for them,
Except when interfered with by the discordant ways of men.

If we observe farming practices down through the ages,
We see giving and receiving till quite recent stages.
Now we see taking, with new and different kinds of force.
The land just keeps on giving, it has to, of course.

Can it stop and say "no" I won't give any more?
This is a scenario we may soon get to explore.
If trees continue to disappear, so will the rain.
Then humanity will enter a new world full of pain.

Global weather events will become ever more severe.
Floods and droughts will be common, on our little blue sphere
Catastrophic events will be occurring much more often,
Unless we can change soon, unless our attitudes can soften.

How then do we change, to a more harmonious type of living?
We need to get back to mutualistic receiving, and giving.
All life is in a balance, it's a delicate sort of dance,
There has to be more respect and maybe even some romance.

The connection between us and the earth, the rain and sun,
Is so important to understand, because it affects everyone.
Its not just for the farmers who farm in all the lands
But even for the city folk, the power is in all our hands.

If we treat our brother as we would like them in turn to treat us,
We are giving what we'd like to receive, and that is definitely a plus.
If we give consciously to the earth, then wait patiently to receive,
It will produce more crops for us than we ever could believe.

Metamorphosis

I am not yet born, I live in a cocoon.
When my body is transformed (and it will be very soon),
You'll see what I am meant to be and you will be in awe.
How different the creature I've become, Is from the one I was before.

This outer cocoon is what I let people see,
But it is only the outward manifestation of me.
Look more carefully if you will, peer deeply inside.
Behind the pretence and the posturing is the place where I hide.
What you see is my shell, my façade, my cocoon.
I can puff it up bigger just like a balloon.
I try to impress you with my complexity and size.
What you don't know though, is that it is only a disguise.

The real me on the inside is small and compact and pure.
I am gaining strength and wisdom so I can endure,
Life on the outside without needing a shell.
I'm not only changing on the inside, soon the outside will as well.
You will know me when I emerge even though I have changed.
My physical appearance will have been rearranged,
But you will recognise my spirit, which is the real me.
Though I am now confined in this shell, I will soon be free.

Starting Over

I didn't fear failure before I failed, because I never thought that I would.
To get back up and try again is the cure, and although I know that I should,
My mind says, wait, you might fail again. Just stay here, you'll be ok.
Somebody else can do it. You're old, and you've had your day.
But sixty is the new forty, my life is now in its prime.
I am older, but wiser than I was before. This is my time to shine.

I may not be able to please everyone, I'm not even going to try.
Please don't stand in my way. Come with me. Of hard work I am not shy.
There may be some who will sit on the side-lines, who don't support me at all.
It is they who will point and criticise and feel more comfortable if I stay small.
I won't listen to the voice of the naysayers, who tell me I'm doing it wrong.
I've done it before and I'll do it again, but this time it won't take me as long.
No longer will I be swayed, by the expert opinions of those
Who, though they have no skin in the game, give advice like someone who knows.

It is I who carry the risk. The decisions are mine to make.
I am a responsible person, I will admit if I make a mistake.
What I once feared to lose, I held tight, in the hope that it would stay.
I will now let go and have faith. I will even give some away.
Though I know financial success will be mine, if indeed it is meant to be.
The lessons I learn on the journey are equally valuable to me.

I have the knowledge inside me, in my hands I hold all the skill.
I have capable helpers beside me, I have determination and will.
This time I know I'll succeed. I will put the fear of failure aside.
I will follow my heart and allow, my own inner wisdom to guide.

Why do I volunteer?

Why do I volunteer at "Windana", an interesting question indeed?
I will try to give you an answer, but I'm not sure if I will succeed.

We don't realize how everything, all works together, for our good.
We take many things for granted, and don't notice, but we should.
For some, life's been a struggle, now you have the chance to change.
"Windana" offers the opportunity for your life to be rearranged.

We are all a part of this community, and for it to function well.
We must work as a team, together, and on this thought we should dwell.
We need to share with each other, what we hide inside our souls.
Our deepest thoughts and aspirations, our fears, our dreams, our goals.
We may not understand the connections we develop while we are here.
But each one is a stepping stone on the path, which someday will be clear.

Some may struggle with the closeness, and need some time on their own,
Others may crave social contact and hate to be left alone.
We come from different backgrounds and we all have differing needs,
But it's clear, we all need to be here, because it's here that we sow new seeds.
The seeds for our new future, the seeds of reform, and of hope.
It's here we learn strategies to enable us, strategies to help us cope.

Most people like to be generous, it makes us all feel good.
I see opportunities to give, all around. I wish that everyone could.
To be generous with our time, a small gift, a hug or a smile.
A kind thought, a touch, or encouragement, to go that extra mile.
There are so many ways to help we don't have to be a volunteer.
But I feel privileged to be allowed, to share my talents here.

A strange thing about gifts is, that you often give the gift that you need.
For instance you may give the gift of books, if you're one who likes to read.
To be generous with your time, especially if you are time poor,
Is a powerful way to increase it, it's strange how you seem to have more.
If you struggle to save money, then share some, as a gift today.
You'll be amazed at how well this works when you have bills to pay.
Are you lacking in self-worth, then do yourself a big favour,
Share your "worth" with someone else, you, may be their lifesaver.

Being able to part with that something, that you hold most dear,
Is the best way I know to get more of it, and you should have no fear,
That if you give it, it will be gone, and for you there won't be enough.
Trust the universe to provide you, with more than you need of the stuff.

Understanding and wisdom are the two things that I desire the most,
So I share with you what little I have, pardon me, if this sounds like I boast.
So what bought me here to "Windana" and not somewhere else instead?
I'm not really sure, perhaps fate, I just feel this is where I've been led.
Try to make use of my talents, and engage with me, while I'm here.
As for me, I'll just follow the path, whenever it shows itself clear.

Country Fire Authority Volunteer

I am just like you, I am a volunteer.
But you are lieutenants and captains with experience, respect and no fear.
I am a little bit lost, I'm not sure which way I should go.
I need you to guide and direct me 'cos I'm new, so how would I know.

Which path should I take to become what you need, is there a plan that is clear?
I want to be helpful, please show me how, because I am a volunteer.
I will put my life on hold whenever a turnout message comes through.
I will put my life on the line to help others in need as you do.

Is there a mentor who'll guide me, to show me which course I should do?
How can I get the right skills to be useful 'cos I want to become just like you?
And when the time comes that I'm useful and there's a vacancy or there's a need,
Let me step up and provide me with support and the knowledge to lead.

Who Am I

While I stand here before you, what do you see,
As you gaze at this manifestation of me?
Do you see grey hair, wrinkles and a fondness for food?
(You could say old and fat, but let's not be rude)

My stature is neither too short nor too tall.
My shoes don't have heels so I'm less likely to fall.
I'm dressed for comfort rather than style.
I've an unadorned face Except for my smile.

My hands are big, my body is strong.
My chin is determined, my toes extra long.
I lack neither confidence nor power of decision.
I have strong intuition and clarity of vision.

Do you see I'm a woman gentle and soft?
Do you see strength and courage and ideals held aloft?
Can you see my emotions in the way that I walk?
And gauge the level of my intellect when I talk.

Do you see only what's visible to the naked eye?
Can you reach any deeper, I invite you to try.
Use all of your senses, observe the essence of me.
Close your eyes and listen, maybe then you will 'see'.

You could ask me about the things that I do,
Although they're not me either, but they'll give you a clue.
My achievements are a reflection of the passion inside,
Check out Facebook and google. No-one can hide.

I'm a wife and a mother of 5 grown up kids,
So far they've had had 6 of their own billy lids.
That makes me a grandma, I love them to pieces.
And I'm an aunt to 31 nephews and nieces.
I'm a sister, a daughter, a friend and a lover.
I'm fortunate to still have a father and mother.

I'm a mentor, a coach, a boss and a teacher.
I'm a farmer, a poet and a peaceful truth seeker.
I meditate daily, I like time on my own.
I love to garden and share the food that I've grown.

I read lots of books, I love learning new things.
I'm grateful for the questions and answers life brings.
According to Meyers –Briggs I'm a dreamer of dreams.
I am ever evolving or that's how it seems.

As a caterpillar from an egg develops and grows,
Metamorphosis occurs and as everyone knows,
A beautiful butterfly waits within,
For a change to take place and its new life to begin.

Who is the real me, I am yet to find out,
And I think that's what our lives are all about.
We cant know the future but we can watch it unfold.
I look forward to metamorphoses as I grow old.

Meditation

I have a strong and healthy body.
I have a quick enquiring mind.
I am wise and understanding.
I am generous and kind.
The one thing I value more highly
Than any one other trait,
Is the wisdom that comes from experience,
For that I will patiently await.

It doesn't come by magic,
Wisdom must be earned.
It comes with understanding,
From reflecting it is learned.
I put aside some time each day,
To sit and quietly meditate.
In this way I enable wisdom to infiltrate.

What If My Thoughts Were The Fruit Of A Tree?

What if my thoughts were the fruit of a tree?
And the tree was my brain, such a small part of me.
If the nerves of my legs branched toward that of my toes,
And joined delicate roots in all ten of those.

And from my neck and my arms the nerves dangled down,
Like an intricate root mass reaching for ground.
How many roots would it take to nourish this tree?
To nourish my brain, to set my thoughts free?

From where comes the food to feed such a thing,
To provide energy, good health and be nourishing.
Though my body is physical, my thoughts flower as spirit.
Sensory input to my brain releases emotions within it.

If my nerves send out flowers along my nerve stem,
Thought fruits will develop, and I can express them.
How do I make my thoughts useful? Please help me to know.
Can the fruit of my brain be used to help others to grow?

Is there a particular soil in which my brain/plant grows best?
One that is deeply enriching so my thoughts aren't distressed?
If I want my tree to produce fruit that is beautiful and wise,
Nourishing to the soul and a delight for the eyes.
Then I should feed it with gratitude for all that I see,
What I feel, taste and hear that is all around me.

With respect for creation and how it all fits together,
With the wonder of cycles, of the moon, sun and weather.
On the cycles of life and how nature evolves,
How every physical thing breaks down and dissolves.
And becomes something new, nothing is lost in the end.
On change constantly occurring, we can depend.

That life is a mystery is no secret to me.
I keep searching for fractals 'cos their truth sets me free.
They're the food that I need to make my thoughts higher.
I seek natural wisdom. That is my strongest desire.

Feeling Attacked

I feel hurt and confused like I'm being attacked.
I'm not sure what I did to get verbally whacked.
I must have done something to make him upset,
I don't feel any guilt but I do feel regret.

Regret for the companionship and comfort we've lost,
For time spent in silence and the emotional cost.
Fear for our future, anger at the past.
Sadness overwhelms me and tears fall at last.

To wash away bitterness, to wash away hate,
To allow forgiveness to creep in before it's too late.
To smooth over the rough spots and patch up the cracks.
Get plenty of practice, because there'll be more attacks.

If issues were discussed it would avoid more confusion,
However changing the subject can create the illusion,
That nothing is wrong, there's no need to discuss,
Just pretend nothing happened, let's not make a fuss.

So nothing improves and nothing is gained,
A relationship not strengthened will always be strained.
No-one is perfect we all have our quirks,
Forbearance and tolerance in a relationship works.

Marriage

When I tell you about something new I learned today,
Please don't get upset and take it the wrong way.
I'm not telling it to you, to make you feel dumb.
The excitement of sharing it makes me succumb.

I love learning new things and I'm sorry you don't,
Or is it just because I told it to you that you won't.
Whatever your reason, it kills any pleasure,
In my sharing with you my nuggets of treasure.

Of what shall we speak then so I don't rock the boat?
Give me some rules of engagement so I can take note,
Of the topics preferred and the ones to avoid.
Believe me, I'm not trying to make you annoyed.

I know that sex is taboo and so is anything clever.
Will your sensitivity reduce or will it continue for ever?
I know that you love me and for that I am grateful.
Is talking to me openly really that hateful?

Would marriage counselling be out of the question?
It may be of some help, they might have a suggestion.
To help me to help you, and for you to help me.
A marriage takes two people I'm sure you'll agree.

Numbing with scotch every night means you're hurting,
But it won't solve the problems around which we are skirting.
What shall we do then, put our head in the sand?
And endure till death parts us, oh isn't love grand.

That's fine for you, but I want more out of life,
I care for you dear, I am your wife.
For thirty six years we've put our marriage on hold,
We need to work on it now before we're too old.

Character Building

Marriage is character building, some would have us believe,
Where two leave their families and together they cleave.
After the honeymoon period is over,
Reality hits, no more romps in the clover.

Our insecurities and old habits come to the fore,
They can be hard to deal with and harder to explore.
We may start to look at each other anew,
No more rose coloured glasses for us to look through.
We can upset each other without even trying,
He might get angry, she might start crying.

He hides in his shed to avoid feeling guilt,
With hidden treasures a mans shed is packed to the hilt.
He can make himself busy, he can stay up there all day,
He knows she is angry but he knows she won't say.
Best to remain busily tinkering. Unaware and alone.
Relationship problems unexplored or unknown.

She simmers like a saucepan on the stovetop,
Not brave enough to speak up or to ask him to stop.
She tidies the house to avoid meeting his eyes,
Afraid he might think her weak if she cries

Silent anger's a poison that erodes marital love,
Like fiery heat that glows scorching down from above.
Sucking moisture from the air till it's too hot to breathe,
While undercurrents of hostility oh so quietly seethe.

If it's too hot it needs quelling before love is dead.
How can this happen when they both hide inside their head?
They each blame the other for what each one is feeling.
If neither addresses the issues, they can't move toward healing.

They both are avoiding what they know they should do.
Can you see what's happening? Do you do this too?
Sometimes I get frustrated and expect more of my spouse.
I'd like help with some fix-it chores around the house.
I get so tired of asking, why can't he see,
His procrastination is really bothering me.

Just one more movie, just a little more sleep,
I'll fix it tomorrow, the problem will keep.
Procrastination, depression? responsibility lacking,
If I say how I feel he might think I'm attacking.

I need to say something, but he should already know.
If I'm too scared to speak up, how will we grow?
Should I cling to my anger because I am right?
Will my bitterness keep our bed warm at night?

Who will make the first move to break down the wall?
What can we both do to help it to fall?
Self-preservation and love can't live together,
It's one or the other, we have to choose whether,
We put ourselves first and thereby live without love,
Or swallow our pride and give our ego a shove.
Both seem hard choices to make, can we defer?
To not choose at all is what most would prefer.

Expecting better results from the save behaviour is crazy.
Not being willing to change to improve is just lazy.
That's what we've been doing and so far it's not working,
Nothing has improved, submerged feelings are still lurking.

This problem is universal, it's why there are wars,
Because instead of forgiving, we are all keeping scores.
To do the best we can with what we have been given,
We must get over our selves to start wholehearted living.

Asking For Money

I hate asking you for money,
Because it seems to make you cranky honey.
To discuss such things is hard for me,
Because from conflict I must flee.
I would not ask but fear I must,
Or this family business will go bust.
I know this is a risk I'M taking,
And it is YOUR piggy bank I'm breaking.
I hesitate to make you cross,
But without your help I'm at a loss.
Repayments can be monthly made,
Until every cent has been repaid.
On my promise you can rely,
Let me tell you now the reason why.
If I die first what's mine is yours,
According to our countries laws.
If you die first you'll never know,
And you won't need it where you go.
I know you'll be waiting for me there,
And forever after for your share.
If you'd prefer repayment in this life,
Then it's a darn good thing that I'm your wife.
Cos if by chance I run out of doe,
Then there's always sex you know.
But to recoup this way I think you might,
Need to increase your appetite.
In anticipation I'm thanking you,
For the money (and sex too).

On Holidays

Here in Japan I'm a kept woman,
I walk him to work each day.
Then I go where I please,
As free as the breeze,
And be back home in time to play.

We eat out at night or watch movies,
Or discover new ways to get lost.
The streets are alive,
And so bright after five,
It's his pleasure to cover the cost.

I've thought about this and I've wondered,
How is this different from home?
He works to pay bills,
While I seek new kinds of thrills,
But at the end we're together alone.

And looking back I pause to reflect,
On the life he's allowed me to lead.
Once the kids all left home,
My time was my own,
But his yoke has never been freed.

I could play or work if I wanted,
When the children went off to school.
But a man has to choose,
To work, or he'll lose,
His purpose in life, that's the rule.

Ten more years to go till retirement,
But his body is starting to wear.
What can I do,
To take the pressure off you?
I will if I can, 'cos I care.

I'd like us to grow old together,
And enjoy whatever time we have left.
Let's conspire and make plans,
Maybe explore other lands,
Before you cross over and leave me bereft.

I Am Your Precious Flower

I am your precious flower,
My scent can make you sneeze.
But for your best enjoyment,
You must let me open please.
My beauty will overwhelm you,
With rare sensory delight.
But only if you're patient,
Can you experience this sight.
Don't get too excited,
And pluck me from the stem.
When my petals are not open,
You'll not enjoy me fully then.
In your haste to fill your senses,
If you pick my bud too early,
You may wonder in the morning,
Why am taciturn and surly.
Remember this exquisite pleasure,
Is at its best when shared.
When we synchronise together,
Our pleasure will be paired.
Don't put me on a pedestal,
Or on the table in a vase.
I know we're from different planets,
Me from Venus, you from Mars.
My flower although precious,
Is only a small part,
Of the plant that I'm attached to,
It is there you'll find my heart.

Greedy Gus

We have a goat called Gus, he is as greedy as can be.
Usually when I call him he races flat out to me.
Not because he's lonely or because he's missed me so,
But because he is a guts, (goats are always hungry you know).

I usually give them food, when I call the animal's to come home.
Gus is smart, the first back gets more, this he's always known.
He can leap a fence or jump a creek, clear anything that's in his sight.
His nose is always first in the feed, he figures it's his right.

He will eat more than his fair share, while the others are on their way.
I often said that he ate so much, that he'd blow up and bust some day.
So last night I couldn't' find Gus, I locked everyone else in their pen.
And I searched everywhere I could think of, until I found him again.

I found him in with the rabbits, polishing off the last of their feed.
He had eaten their whole container, which is way more than he could need.
Gus has always been a big eater, but this greediness just left me in awe.
He's struggling to move today though 'cos his belly's a little bit sore.

Perhaps he's now learned his lesson, and will keep his appetite under control.
Hopefully he will be able to confine himself, to the food that I put in his bowl.

Cheeky Frog

Buddy is a chubby pug,
He is my husband's dog.
He has to share his water bowl,
With a cheeky green tree frog.

Fluffy as we named him,
Lives behind the fridge.
There's not much room behind there,
But he only needs a smidge.

He comes out late at night,
Covered in dust and hair and stuff.
And jumps into the dog bowl,
To wash off all the fluff.

Buddy doesn't seem to mind,
He seems happy enough to share.
His water bowl with a frog,
Even when it's full of dust and hair.

It would be a different story though,
If Fluffy ate dog food.
I know that Buddy wouldn't like that much,
He would consider that quite rude.

Printed in the United States
By Bookmasters